AF228151

MODERN
FARMING

Essential Library
An Imprint of Abdo Publishing
abdobooks.com

ABDOBOOKS.COM

Published by Abdo Publishing, a division of ABDO, PO Box 398166, Minneapolis, Minnesota 55439. Copyright © 2025 by Abdo Consulting Group, Inc. International copyrights reserved in all countries. No part of this book may be reproduced in any form without written permission from the publisher. Essential Library™ is a trademark and logo of Abdo Publishing.

Printed in China.
102024
012025

Cover Photo: Thomas Trutschel/Photothek/Getty Images (front); Shutterstock Images (back)
Interior Photos: Thomas Trutschel/Photothek/Getty Images, 1; recep-bg/E+/Getty Images, 5; Michael Macor/San Francisco Chronicle/Hearst Newspapers/Getty Images, 7; Chris Ratcliffe/Bloomberg/Getty Images, 8; Zhou Yi/China News Service/Getty Images, 14–15; Jair F. Coll/Bloomberg/Getty Images, 17, 20; Dennis Kunkel Microscopy/Science Source, 22; Brendan Smialowski/AFP/Getty Images, 25; Shutterstock Images, 26, 29, 33, 37 (crops), 37 (satellite), 37 (computer), 37 (tractor), 51, 57, 60, 82; Henrik A. Jonsson/Shutterstock Images, 37 (ground station); Ashley Cooper/Construction Photography/Avalon/Hulton Archive/Getty Images, 38; Kyodo News Stills/Getty Images, 41; Nina Liashonok/Ukrinform/Future Publishing/Getty Images, 45; Christinne Muschi/Bloomberg/Getty Images, 48; Sean Gallup/Getty Images News/Getty Images, 49; Costfoto/NurPhoto/Getty Images, 54, 75; Bernd Wüstneck/dpa-Zentralbild/picture alliance/Getty Images, 63; Julian Stratenschulte/dpa/picture alliance/Getty Images, 66; Guido Kirchner/dpa/picture alliance/Getty Images, 69; Buddhika Weerasinghe/Bloomberg/Getty Images, 70; Andrea DiCenzo/Getty Images News/Getty Images, 78; John Hart/Wisconsin State Journal/AP Images, 85; DC Studio/Shutterstock Images, 87; Andia/Universal Images Group/Getty Images, 90; Jacob Mathers/Shutterstock Images, 93; Paul Morigi/Getty Images for Common Ground/Getty Images Entertainment/Getty Images, 97

Editors: Kari Cornell and Arnold Ringstad
Series Designer: Maggie Villaume

Library of Congress Control Number: 2024938301

PUBLISHER'S CATALOGING-IN-PUBLICATION DATA
Names: Wheeler, Jill C., author.
Title: Modern farming / by Jill C. Wheeler
Description: Minneapolis, Minnesota: ABDO Publishing, 2025 | Series: Fascinating food | Includes online resources and index.
Identifiers: ISBN 9781098295318 (lib. bdg.) | ISBN 9798384916314 (ebook)
Subjects: LCSH: Food crops--Biotechnology--Juvenile literature. | Locally produced foods--Juvenile literature. | Slow food movement--Juvenile literature. | Food supply--Juvenile literature. | Garden farming--Juvenile literature. | Urban farming--Juvenile literature. | Mechanized farming--Juvenile literature.
Classification: DDC 630.20--dc23

CONTENTS

A CROP TAKES SHAPE

A spring morning dawns with a ping from a smartphone. Satellite imagery, weather data, and long-range forecasting models indicate several good weather days for corn planting lie ahead. A farmer does a quick check of the soil temperature in the field, then grabs a tablet to access the farm management software (FMS) for a closer look.

Detailed information on the prepurchased hybrid corn seed, its GMO trait package, and its seed treatment have already been entered into the FMS. The system's algorithms inform the farmer when moisture levels in the field are too high or too low. The FMS suggests adjustments to the in-furrow fertilizer that will be applied. After that, it's time to go.

The farmer climbs into the tractor cab and starts the Global Positioning System (GPS) receiver, which

An array of advanced agricultural hardware and software has changed the way farms operate, making them more productive and efficient.

pins the current location of the tractor and loads the field's location boundaries. The field's topography, soil types, and historical yield data have already been used within the FMS to calculate the optimal number of plants per acre. Soil assessments collected from laboratory tests and data from previous harvests allow the farmer to apply fertilizer only where it is most needed.

The farmer nears the field and switches the controls to the autosteer function. Autosteer uses the tractor's GPS receiver along with permanent base stations on the farm that correct the GPS signal to make location data even more precise. This allows the farmer to drive a line that is straight down to the inch, ensuring the proper application of seed, crop protection products, or nutrients.

The farmer remembers how exhausting it was keeping rows straight before autosteer. Autosteer also makes each pass across the field as efficient as possible. This saves money on costly crop inputs and fuel while reducing greenhouse gas emissions.

The steering is automated, leaving the farmer free to focus on what else is happening in the field. Today things are running smoothly, and each time the farmer looks back to check on the planter, everything is working as planned.

From time to time, the farmer also reviews the plan for the field on his tablet and gets updates on corn prices from his smartphone. There's even time to de-stress by watching a few videos.

Each year, the farmer has just one chance to plant, grow, and harvest a crop as efficiently as possible. The cost of seeds, fertilizer, and other inputs usually increases each year, while the price the farmer receives for the corn produced is unpredictable and may even drop below the cost of production. This means it's important for the farmer to use only what's needed and apply it as precisely as possible to avoid waste.

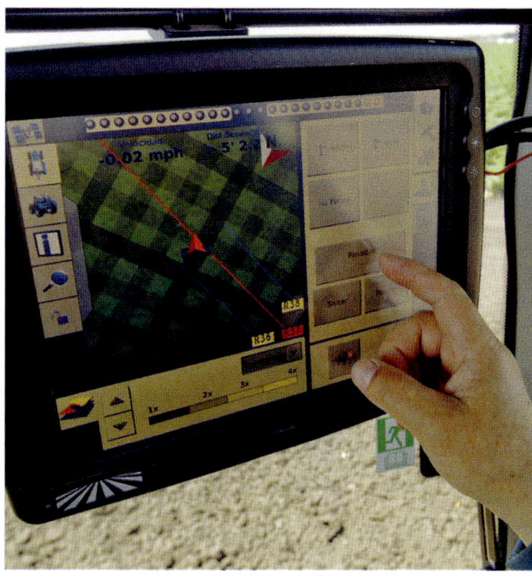

GPS receivers were built into tractors starting in the 1990s, and they have since become a standard feature.

ASSESSING AND ADAPTING

The farmer keeps an eye on the crop as the seeds emerge and the seedlings begin to grow. The FMS gathers data from soil moisture sensors, satellite imagery, and weather forecasts. This information is used to guide the irrigation

Displays inside modern combines allow farmers to study data about their harvest while they gather the crops.

system, determining when automated sprinklers turn on and how long they run. Running them too often or at the wrong time wastes energy and water.

In early summer, the system's visual reports and historical patterns indicate weeds are beginning to compete with the young crop. The farmer gets in the tractor and uses GPS to precisely guide the application of an herbicide. This substance kills the weeds but not the crop, which has been genetically modified to tolerate it. Advances in pesticide technology mean the farmer needs just ounces of the herbicide per acre of land.

A few weeks later, humidity and temperatures raise a disease alert in the FMS. The farmer contacts a local adviser, who arrives at the farm with a drone that's programmed to identify areas of potential disease. Using imaging technology similar to what's used on spy satellites, the drone autonomously flies over the farm, taking thousands of images to be analyzed by computers. An artificial intelligence (AI) system reviews the images and helps make a recommendation. A fungicide treatment is needed to help control a fungal disease that is destroying the plants' leaves. The adviser returns to the farm with a different drone that sprays the infected plants that were identified earlier. The fungicide spray treats the diseased plants and stops the condition from spreading to other plants.

As fall arrives, the farmer relies on experience, data from the FMS, and visits to the field to determine when the crop is ready to harvest. When weather and field conditions are good, the farmer readies the combine, which has its own GPS and yield monitoring system. Driving through the fields on autosteer, the farmer can see real-time data on which parts of the field produced better yields. The farmer makes mental notes of which areas should be investigated for potential changes next year.

When the crop has been harvested and stored, the farmer will add those insights to data in the FMS. The system then makes adjustments to the amounts of next year's seed, fertilizer, and crop protection products. Meanwhile, sensors and AI systems automatically adjust the fans inside the bins where the grain is stored to control the humidity and help prevent the grain from spoiling. The systems keep the stored grain in good condition until the farmer transfers it to the buyer. This could be for a year or longer.

HIGH-TECH HARVESTS

The process of growing crops and raising livestock has changed dramatically in the course of human history. Agriculture has moved through three distinct revolutions, beginning with the Neolithic Revolution. The Neolithic marked the change from nomadic hunter-gatherer lifestyles to settled farming communities, where people cultivated crops and raised domestic animals for food. Early farmers came up with ways to better harness the natural tools of water, sunlight, and soil. For example, early farmers discovered that rotating the crops grown on their fields from year to year improved soil quality and increased yields.

The second agricultural revolution involved key labor-saving technologies developed in the 1700s and 1800s. Among these were the seed drill in 1701, which allowed for more efficient and uniform planting. The threshing machine, introduced in 1786, made harvests more efficient. And the self-polishing plow, developed in 1837, allowed farmers to better prepare the heavy soils of the midwestern United States.

This era also saw the first self-propelled tractor and combine. This machine was named for its ability to combine the jobs of cutting crops, threshing the grain, and winnowing it from the chaff. The combine was patented in 1887, and the first self-propelled tractor followed in 1892. Moving to motorized vehicles rather than equipment pulled by horses, oxen, or mules reduced labor needs on the farm

CYRUS McCORMICK'S REAPER

The horse-drawn mechanical reaper ranks among the most important agricultural innovations of the second agricultural revolution. Developed in 1831 by American Cyrus McCormick, the reaper mechanized the process of harvesting small grains, such as wheat. The machine featured a reel to gather the grain, a blade to cut it, and a platform to stack it. Prior to the reaper, harvesting grain required several people to do the job by hand. If a farmer could not get enough laborers at harvest time, the grain might rot in the field.

American plant scientist Norman Borlaug is credited with starting the green revolution. Borlaug won a grant to create higher-yielding wheat varieties for farmers in Mexico who were facing hunger and malnutrition due to crop failures caused by wheat diseases. Borlaug developed a shorter, sturdier variety of wheat that was better able to remain upright, even when better fertilization and watering techniques led to more kernels on the head, making it heavier. Upright grain tends to stay dry, whereas grain that falls to the ground can become moist and develop mold or mildew issues. In 1970, Borlaug received the Nobel Peace Prize for his work, which is estimated to have prevented a billion deaths from malnutrition worldwide.[2]

and made larger farms more feasible. Farming also became a slightly less physically demanding occupation.

The green revolution began in the mid-1900s. It focused on reducing global hunger by increasing the productivity of two of the world's major food crops: rice and wheat. This revolution involved the use of selective breeding in plants to create new seed varieties, along with more widespread use of irrigation and synthetic fertilizers.

Since the 2010s, farming has been in the midst of a fourth revolution. This revolution is harnessing advanced technologies such as cloud computing, genetic engineering, and AI to produce food as efficiently as possible. At the same time, there are elements of farming that can't be controlled, including the weather, photosynthesis, and the basics of animal reproduction. However, technology can be used to develop plant varieties and animal breeds that grow at a faster rate. In 1925, it took chickens an average of 112 days to reach their market weight of 2.5 pounds (1.1 kg). In 2023, chickens took just 47 days to reach a market weight of more than 6.5 pounds (3 kg).[3]

Like animal reproduction, growing seasons cannot be controlled or easily extended. Technology can help farmers plan ahead. Azahar Ali teaches animal sciences and biological systems engineering at Virginia Tech. Ali says, "Combined, smart devices and AI also offer the potential for predictive analysis, enabling producers to proactively anticipate challenges such as disease outbreaks and weather patterns."[4]

Modern farmers must also adapt to changes in global markets and the environment as both geopolitics and climate become more unpredictable. The current global food system is being scrutinized for its negative impacts on society, nature, and the environment. But Lukas Fricke is one

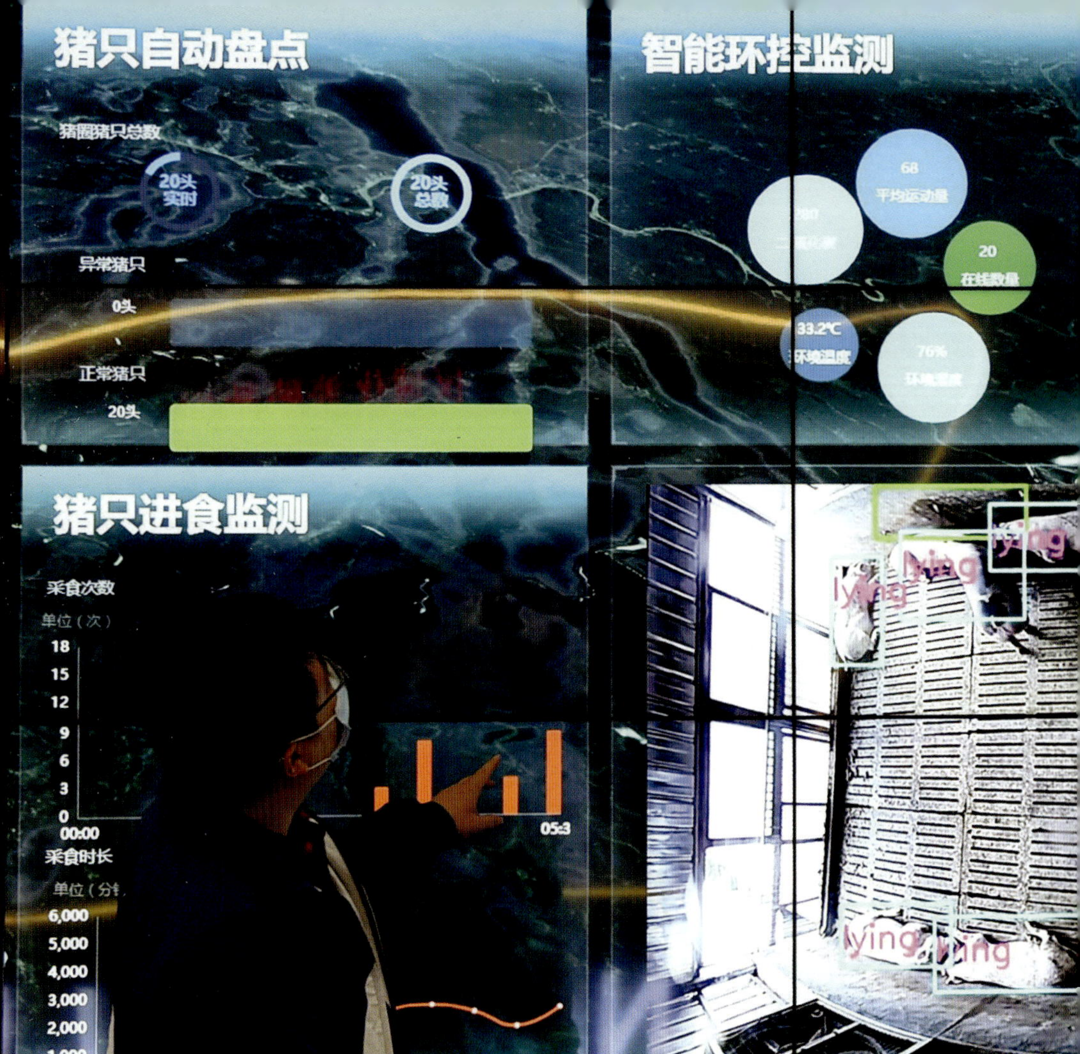

At a high-tech pig farm in China, real-time data is displayed on a large screen.

farmer who is using technology to farm more sustainably.

Fricke is a pork farmer who works with his brothers to run Union Farms in Ulysses, Nebraska. He says, "Working with technology partners and trading partners . . . helps us realize the benefits of our sustainability efforts up and down the supply chain. By allowing sustainability information to flow

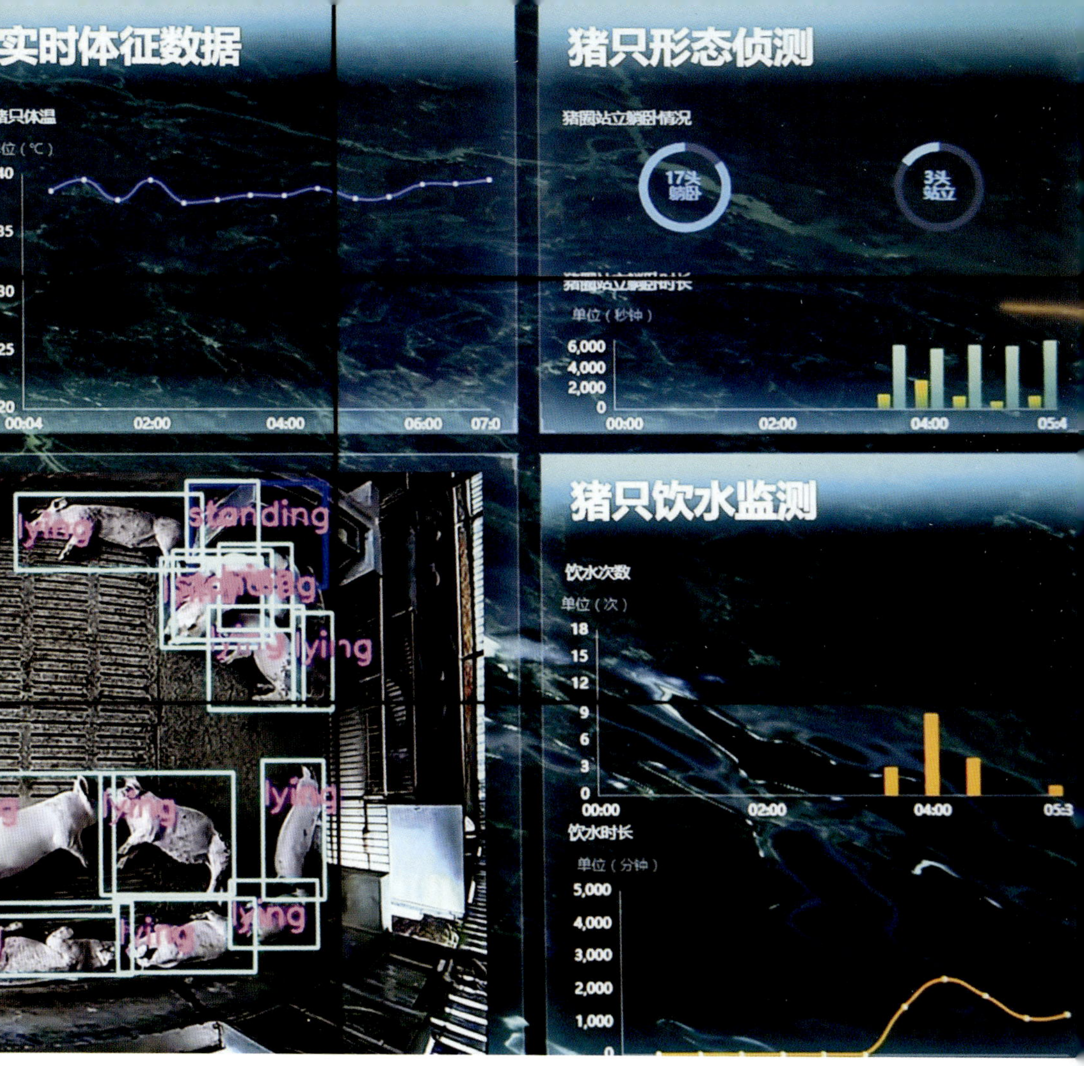

with the supply chain, downstream producers can help show what they are doing on the farm to make a better environment and world."[6] Addressing environmental and other concerns requires innovation and cooperation at all stages in the food industry.

CHAPTER TWO

HYBRID GENETICS AND GMOs

Deciding which seeds to plant is one of the most important decisions farmers must make each year. Seed genetics plays a major role in determining yield potential and how well a crop stands up to environmental challenges such as drought, plant diseases, and insect pests. While some crops, such as tree or vine crops, produce annual harvests for many years, most row-crop farmers must purchase new seeds each year. That gives seed companies an opportunity to improve their seeds year after year.

Changing the DNA makeup of seeds is called genetic modification. Humans have been genetically modifying seeds for hundreds of years. However, the way this is done has changed dramatically. Early humans learned to save seeds from their best performing plants to use the following year. If early farmers had a plant that appeared to resist a

Seed genetics researchers are developing ways to help
important crops survive in the world's changing climate.

particular disease, they saved the seeds from that plant to help protect yields against that disease the next year.

Later, seed researchers began crossbreeding different types of plants from the same species. For example, a plant breeder who had found a corn plant that resisted disease might save some of its seeds and cross-pollinate those plants with seedlings from a corn plant that had performed well during drier seasons. The resulting cross may resist both disease and drought. This process of combining different parent types to create a new plant that shares similar traits of both parent plants is called hybridization.

Crossbreeding brought new genetic diversity to seed options and made for better crops. Hybrid plants tend to be healthier than inbred plants. This is called hybrid vigor. Plant breeders still harness genetic diversity to improve crop performance, and new tools have sped up the process.

PREDICTING BETTER PLANTS

In the past, developing new seed products has taken a lot of time—often seven to ten years in the case of a new hybrid for corn, the most commonly grown crop in the United States.[2] Much of that time was needed to grow out seeds, examine the resulting plants, record their health and performance, and measure their yield in all the environments in which that plant might grow. In this way, plant breeders could learn how different genetic packages performed around the world and select the best hybrid plants. This process, called phenotyping, is among the most time- and labor-intensive aspects of developing new crop varieties.

Increasingly, modern seed breeding relies on computers for their ability to collect and analyze large amounts of data. Advanced computing capabilities now allow seed breeders to determine the best-performing plants more efficiently. Computers make it possible to quickly analyze decades of information collected on thousands of acres of seed production.

Modern imaging technologies enable computers to quickly analyze digital images of plants to learn what human breeders have in the past had to observe and record plant by plant. Predictive analytics can estimate potential results of crossing certain parent seeds. This method calculates the most likely outcome by using a machine learning model and

other tools to analyze data from similar environments and conditions. Breeders can then save time and resources by choosing only the most promising combinations to bring to the lab, greenhouse, or field.

GENETICALLY MODIFIED ORGANISMS (GMOs)

Modifying a plant's genetics through pollination can go only so far in creating crops that are better able to withstand weather, pests, and diseases. Sometimes the solution involves genetic material from another source. One of the most common ways to control insects in plants relies on

DNA not originally found in plants. Instead, the technology relies on naturally occurring soil bacteria that were first discovered in the early 1900s.

Bacillus thuringiensis, or *Bt*, is toxic to moths that feed on crops such as field corn, tobacco, eggplants, cotton, and sweet corn. This bacterium was discovered in 1901 by a Japanese biologist who was investigating a disease that had been killing silkworms. Though *Bt* is deadly to these specific insects, it does not harm humans or natural predators of those insects, such as birds.

Researchers learned how to create pesticides from *Bt* in the early part of the 1900s. For years, farmers sprayed *Bt* on their crops to prevent insect damage. Yet spraying required time and labor, and it could be washed off the

HOW GMOs SAVED THE PAPAYA

Papaya ringspot virus is the most common and destructive disease affecting papayas. It is found in virtually all papaya-producing regions, but it became an especially serious problem in Hawaii, where the crop is a large part of the state's economy. Hawaiian officials feared the loss of this valuable crop, so in 1985 they funded research into a genetically modified version of the fruit that could resist the devastating disease. The project succeeded, and the virus-resistant Rainbow papaya was approved for planting in 1998. After widespread adoption of the new variety, Hawaiian papaya production recovered to pre-virus levels.

plants by rain. Innovative researchers began to ask if there was a way to get plants to produce the toxic substance in *Bt* on their own.

Early efforts at genetic engineering used multiple processes. One involved exposing organisms to radiation in the hope that the resulting random mutations would include desirable changes. The Ruby Red grapefruit received its deep red color from such a mutation. Another process involved coating particles of gold with genetic material and shooting the particles into the plant at high velocity. With this gene gun, some of the genetic material could be inserted into the cells of plants as the gold particles traveled through them. The plant would then begin to incorporate the new material into its cells.

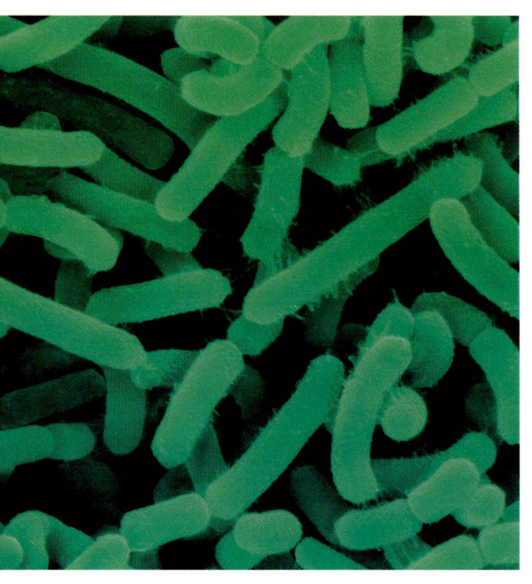

Like many bacteria, *A. tumefaciens* has a rodlike shape.

A more natural solution came from the soil bacterium *Agrobacterium tumefaciens*. For millions of years, *A. tumefaciens* had been inserting its own DNA into plants in the form of galls, or tumors, such as the large lumps often found at the bottoms of trees. Galls can also form on other plants such as rose bushes. Humans identified *A. tumefaciens* as the cause of crown gall disease, which causes the plant tumors, in the early 1900s.

It wasn't until the early 1980s that researchers were able to determine how *A. tumefaciens* was doing its own genetic engineering. Scientists learned how to remove the genes that cause crown gall disease and replace them with bacterial genes, such as *Bt*, to produce the desired traits. By the mid-1990s, farmers could plant seeds containing *Bt* proteins. Target insects feeding on those plants quickly fell ill, stopped feeding, and died.

Genetic modification has since been used to address a host of challenges in modern farming and food handling.

SAVING LIVES WITH GMO INSULIN

Insulin has saved millions of lives since its discovery as a treatment for diabetes in the early 1920s. Insulin originally was manufactured from cow and pig organs. While it saved lives, it also created allergic reactions in some patients. In the late 1970s, scientists invented synthetic insulin, which was produced using a process known as recombinant DNA. Scientists used genetic modification to insert the human gene that produces insulin into *E. coli* bacteria. As the bacteria rapidly replicated, they produced insulin that had a similar chemical makeup to the human version.

In row-crop farming, GMOs are used primarily to prevent insect damage and allow for easier and more effective weed control. In vegetables, crops such as squash have been modified to resist destructive viruses. Apples and potatoes now have genetically modified versions specifically to prevent the browning of cut produce that leads to food waste.

GMOs quickly proved themselves popular and effective. At the same time, they were expensive and time-consuming to create. A single GMO trait can require more than $115 million in investment and an average development time of more than 16 years to pass all required research, testing, and regulatory approvals.[3] Fortunately for farmers and consumers, a new technology arrived to enable even more precise modifications of nature's offerings.

GENE EDITING

By the early 2000s, researchers had access to a collection of new tools for genetic engineering through a process called gene editing. Gene editing allows scientists to more precisely insert, remove, or modify the DNA within a particular gene to add a new trait without the need for multiple generations of crossing one plant with another.

Dr. Mary-Dell Chilton

Mary-Dell Chilton was born in Indianapolis, Indiana, in 1939. She discovered a love for science in high school, when she scored far above average on a test. She attended the University of Illinois to study physics but earned bachelor's and doctorate degrees in chemistry instead. Chilton explains, "In physics, they seemed to know all the answers. . . . But in chemistry I could see things needing to be done."[4]

Eventually Chilton and her husband moved to Saint Louis, Missouri. Chilton helped create her own job at Washington University, where she led a team that developed the first genetically modified plants. They used a natural DNA transfer method involving *A. tumefaciens*. She remembers making a key discovery. "I . . . was performing the calculations at my kitchen table after the kids had gone to bed. I said, 'My God, the DNA is there!' Before that experiment, I was sure that you could not get bacterial genes to recombine with plant genes. . . . But in the process of trying to prove the idea wrong, I proved it was indeed right."[5]

In 1983, Chilton took a job with agriculture firm Ciba-Geigy AG to found its biotechnology research lab. Her work focused on new and improved ways to insert new genes into plants. Chilton received the World Food Prize in 2013 for her contributions to agriculture.

As plant breeders evaluate plants, they can identify specific characteristics or functions and tie them to a particular gene. For example, they might identify a plant that has an unusually high tolerance for dry conditions. Scientists can then use gene editing to edit the DNA of a plant that is more sensitive to drought conditions and make that plant more tolerant to drought. Unlike GMOs, gene editing focuses on genetic material already present in a particular plant species.

Gene editing is becoming increasingly important as scientists work to develop new plant varieties that are better able to grow in a changing climate. Changes in the growing environment, such as higher temperatures, more or less rain, and insect or disease presence, can result in new stresses to a plant. How well a plant responds to those stresses is determined by its genetics and how the genes interact with the environment. Researchers used gene editing to create cacao plants with stronger immune systems to better fight off a disease attacking the plants. Cacao plants are the source of the main ingredient in chocolate.

Gene editing also is being used to modify foods for human consumption. Researchers created a type of wheat that is easier to digest for people with celiac disease. This disease involves an immune reaction to gluten, a protein in wheat. In another project, gene editing was used to turn off the gene that causes mushrooms to turn brown, thus extending their shelf life in stores.

GMO DRAWBACKS

GMOs do have drawbacks. They are relatively new, so effects on humans and the environment are not yet known. For example, if genes from a nut plant are combined with soybean plants, people who have a nut allergy may react to products made with those soybeans. Some GMOs are resistant to antibiotics, so people question if consuming them could make humans resistant as well. GMOs could cross-pollinate with other crops and plants. This could lead to less plant diversity.

CHAPTER THREE

PRECISION AGRICULTURE

Producing crops requires farmers to manage complex biological systems. They must oversee many variables, including soil type and nutrient content, seeds, weather, pests, and diseases. These factors differ across regions and can even vary within a single field. For example, some soils within a field may easily absorb a heavy rain, while other parts of the same field may flood. Some parts of a field may have all the nutrients needed for a crop at planting, while others cannot support a healthy crop without added fertilizer.

Early farmers identified many of these differences and adapted their management practices when farming was largely manual. As farm sizes grew and mechanized equipment came into use, farmers had less time and opportunity to learn and selectively manage these nuances within

Today's farming technology can gather a wide assortment
of data about the unique attributes of each farmer's fields
and use that information to maximize productivity.

their fields. Precision agriculture helps modern farmers regain this knowledge and more effectively manage these many variables.

Precision agriculture technologies include GPS, sensors and other data collection systems, specialized software for recordkeeping and mapping, and satellite imagery. These tools help farmers grow more crops with fewer workers, deal with changing environmental conditions, and cope with the rising costs of seed and fertilizer.

Precision agriculture began in the early 1990s with the development of the first yield monitor. This tool measured the amount of grain that entered a grain tank during harvesting, allowing farmers to see crop yields in real time as they passed over their fields during harvest. The monitors worked with a GPS system to help farmers see which parts of their fields were performing the best and which parts needed attention. Often, the new information came as a surprise. Lee Kline, a popular farm radio broadcaster, remembered watching a yield monitor fluctuate from

179 bushels of corn per acre to just 35 and back to 169, all in the same field.[2] GPS and mapping capabilities were soon added to yield monitors. Farmers could then print and analyze a precise map of each field and address problems the following crop year.

Collecting, storing, and analyzing data from multiple crop years created the need for ways to manage the information. This led to the development of specialized farm management software (FMS) systems. These systems help farmers and their advisers analyze large volumes of field data and make recommendations for management changes. Data for these systems can come from farm machinery, such as yield monitors on harvesting machines. It can also come from sensors in the fields, or the farmer can enter it by hand.

RURAL BROADBAND

A 2020 study found that more than 20 percent of rural US residents lack access to reliable broadband internet service. In urban areas, roughly 1.5 percent of people lack access.[3] This lack of connectivity presents an obstacle to many parts of daily farm life, including distance learning, telehealth opportunities, and adoption of precision farming technologies. Funding for broadband access is increasing, but experts point to a lack of funding coordination and a patchwork of different internet providers as barriers to fixing the problem.

SENSORS AND IMAGERY

The first step in a precision agriculture system is to understand what is happening in each field at a specific time. Farmers can gather this information in several ways, including by visual observation, soil and plant-tissue testing, and monitoring sensors. Sensors in modern agriculture collect data on weather conditions, plant health, soil conditions, and the amount of nutrients in the soil. Sensors are able to collect more data at a faster rate than traditional soil and tissue testing, which required sending samples to a lab for analysis. Modern sensors can be handheld for on-the-spot information or mounted on farm equipment to generate data on the go.

Sensors have become an important tool for managing crop nutrients, such as nitrogen. Nitrogen is one of three critical plant nutrients, along with phosphorus and potassium. Nitrogen is expensive for farmers, and if not used properly, it can wash off fields and pollute water systems. In the early 1990s, researchers began experimenting with different ways to help farmers better monitor and manage their nitrogen use to prevent these problems. This led to the development of probe-type sensors that can measure nitrogen, phosphorus, and potassium levels in the soil.

Handheld sensors can give farmers instant feedback on soil conditions.

When combined with mapping technology, the sensor readings help farmers see where they may need additional nutrients as they prepare for planting.

Sensors are being used in livestock operations as well. For example, solar-powered sensors let farmers know if they are running low on feed. These sensors allow for better management of available feed to keep animals from going hungry while reducing the potential for overfilling bins and wasting feed. Poultry producers can gain valuable information through a camera system that pairs with AI to estimate the weight of each bird, helping producers harvest them at the most efficient time.

Modern farmers are also able to assess nutrient levels while plants are growing to efficiently manage the nutrients plants need. Sensors for this data rely on spectral imagery, measuring the light reflected off the plant

BRIGHT FUTURE FOR AG TECH CAREERS

The agricultural workforce of tomorrow will need dramatically different skills than in the past. This will include AI and machine-learning specialists, data analysts and scientists, and agricultural equipment operators. Agriculture will need many workers in these roles to operate a growing system of on-farm sensors and precision agriculture systems, as well as managing and interpreting the millions of data points they generate.

to determine the levels of chlorophyll, the compound that gives plants their green color. These sensors can be added to farm equipment that applies fertilizers, allowing the sensors to tell the equipment in real time whether more nitrogen is needed within a field. This combination of sensors and application equipment is called variable rate technology (VRT).

SATELLITE DATA

The United States Department of Agriculture (USDA) operates a network of satellites to provide remotely sensed data for agricultural use. The satellites measure the sunlight reflected from plants. How much of this energy is reflected depends upon the health of the plant. Plants under stress, such as those getting too much or not enough water, will reflect different amounts of light than healthy plants. Data from the satellites is transmitted to a station on the ground, where it is collected, analyzed, and mapped.

Satellite images have many uses in agriculture. The data can identify areas of drought, disease, insect infestations, wind or hail damage, overgrazing, nutrient deficiencies, and weed infestations. The data can also be integrated into VRT systems to treat specific problem areas.

ADOPTION AND CHALLENGES

Precision agriculture technologies have helped farmers work efficiently and save money. Very large farming operations are the most likely to use precision agriculture. Large operations are better able to absorb the costs of setting up and running the technology than small farms. Because big operations' many fields are spread out over a large area, they are more likely to have greater variability in soils, so precision agriculture offers the most benefits to this type of business. Additionally, large operations can afford to hire people who can focus on the high-tech skills required for data management and automation.

Adoption rates on smaller farms aren't nearly as high. A 2023 USDA survey found that just 27 percent of US farms

WATER CHALLENGES

Agriculture is the world's largest water consumer. Agricultural water use continues to grow even as global water insecurity rises due to increased demand and strained supply. By 2040, about 40 percent of irrigated agriculture production will be threatened by water stress.[4] Irrigation innovations can help. One example is replacing flood irrigation with more efficient systems, such as drip irrigation. Flood irrigation involves flooding a field with water and letting it soak into the crop. Drip irrigation uses plastic pipes filled with holes that are laid along crop rows to water plants. Farmers can also focus on improving soil health so the water can more easily enter the earth.

REMOTE SENSING

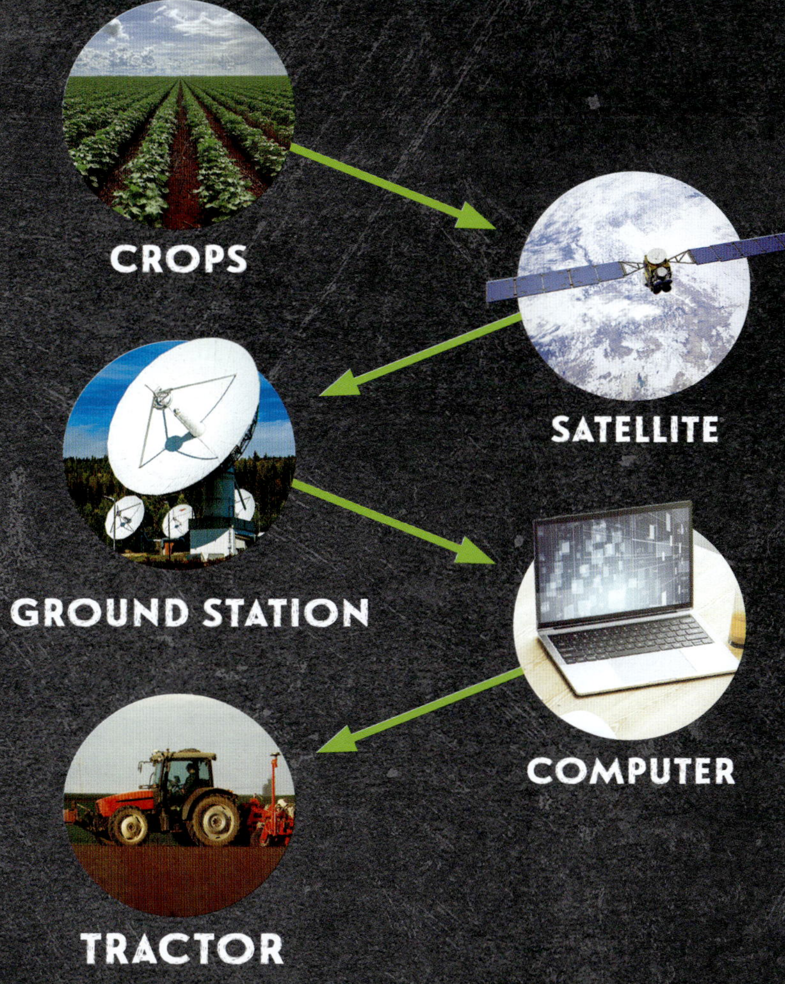

Using remotely sensed data on a farm involves multiple steps. First, a satellite observes the crops and collects data. Then it transmits that data to a ground station. Next, a computer analyzes that data. Finally, the data is presented to the farmer on maps on a tractor's display screens.

Real-time kinematic technology is used for land surveying in addition to agriculture.

and ranches were using these technologies. Midwestern row-crop operations used these technologies the most, with adoption rates in many states at around 50 percent.[5] This is in part because of accuracy issues. While GPS can offer accurate readings within two to three feet (0.6–0.9 m) of a specific point, agricultural needs are more precise. Accuracy within inches is needed to place nutrients in a furrow.

To solve this issue, farmers can install real-time kinematic (RTK) technology. This uses a ground station that helps correct GPS data to make it more precise. But this technology is expensive. Installing an RTK station can cost around $9,000. Farmers can instead pay $1,500 or more for an annual subscription that lets them access an existing station.[6] This is just one of many technologies used to make the farmer's job easier. New farm machinery is improving efficiency as well.

CHAPTER FOUR

MODERN FARM EQUIPMENT

Basic on-farm tasks have not changed much over the years. Crops must be planted, tended, and harvested. Animals must be fed and cared for. Modern farm equipment reflects two major shifts in how those jobs get done: scale and technology.

Large-scale farms account for roughly 3 percent of all US farms, but they represent more than half the total output.[1] Managing large farms requires bigger equipment and more mechanization. While smaller farms may use four-row planters for seeding crops, a large farm may need a 48-row planter to cover more acres in the same amount of time. These larger pieces of equipment cost significantly more and require more powerful tractors to pull them.

Modern farm equipment has made it possible for a family farm business to operate at larger sizes than ever before. A greater challenge can be the mental

A Japanese farmer drives a tractor alongside an autonomous robotic tractor during a 2016 demonstration.

load farmers face during planting and harvest times, when work must be done within a specific time frame. Missing a planting window or harvesting a crop too late can be costly. New technologies can help farmers complete work quickly and efficiently, with less physical and mental stress.

GRAIN STORAGE

The ability to store grain to sell later offers more profit opportunities than selling at harvest, when prices tend to be lower. More than half of the grain stored in the United States is stored at the farm.[2] Stored grain must be dried to prevent spoiling, and grains continue to dry over time. Drier grain weighs less, so farmers may have fewer pounds to sell after months of storage. Farmers balance the price they receive from a delayed sale with the costs of drying and storage.

RTK AUTOSTEER TECHNOLOGY

In 1984, the National Aeronautics and Space Administration (NASA) worked with researchers at Stanford University to develop a system that would improve the location accuracy of GPS technology. The result was RTK technology, which was first used to help NASA control the movement and location of spacecraft. Researchers quickly realized there were many potential applications for RTK. It was incorporated into autosteer for tractors starting in 1999.

RTK autosteer meant farmers could now plant, fertilize, and harvest in rows with accuracy to within an inch (2.5 cm). Autosteer allowed farmers to keep an eye on what else was happening in the field and watch the yield monitor. The technology led to more accurate placement of crops where they could be most productive.

Farmers could avoid accidents that reduced yields, such as driving over crop rows or digging up crops too early. The technology also allowed farmers to expand their windows of time, as they no longer had to rely on daylight for accurate in-field work. A 2019 USDA study found that autosteer technology was being used on 40 percent of all US farm and ranch production acres.[3]

In the early 2020s, fully autonomous tractors complete with GPS, AI-guided obstacle detection sensors, and remote monitoring capabilities became available. Some farmers are now using these advanced machines, which can cost $500,000 or more.[4] These smart tractors can be operated using a smartphone or tablet. Sensors collect and use data for precision agriculture applications, such as mapping and VRT. Unlike human drivers, who get tired, the machines can operate continuously. These smart tractors help address on-farm labor shortages and offer new options to help farmers with disabilities.

There are some drawbacks to adopting autonomous tractors and harvesting machines. In addition to the high cost, autonomous tractors have a steep learning curve that may not be appealing to all farmers. Some of these tractors are powered by electricity rather than fossil fuels, but the electric versions need to be powerful enough to pull large, heavy farm implements such as planters and tillage equipment over the field. That is difficult to achieve with electric motors. These barriers suggest farmers are more likely to invest in add-ons to automate existing equipment instead of purchasing completely new autonomous equipment.

DRONES

Drones have found a niche in modern farming, where they can do many precision jobs. Drones can be equipped with tanks and application systems to spray specific areas for weeds, diseases, and insects. Unlike traditional methods

Large drones can carry several gallons of pesticides at once, delivering it to particular spots in a field.

such as crop dusting that treat entire fields, drones allow farmers to treat only those areas where there is a problem. In one hour, smaller drones can spray about 10 acres (4 ha), while larger ones can treat up to 50 acres (20 ha) per hour.[6]

Some drones are outfitted with multispectral cameras, which can identify plant health issues even before they are visible to human eyes. Multispectral cameras take in types of light beyond what humans can see, including infrared and ultraviolet light, to analyze fields and create maps. When equipped with zoom lenses, these cameras can easily focus to the level of individual plants or field features. Crop insurance companies are beginning to use drones to survey fields after storms, helping them process insurance claims. High-resolution thermal imaging also can be added to drones. With this technology, drones can track the location of livestock any time of day by sensing body heat.

Drones for farming can range in cost from several thousand dollars to around $30,000.[7] Some agricultural retailers offer drone services to area farmers. This makes the technology available to smaller farms that might not have the necessary resources to use their own drones.

ROBOTICS

Dairy production is among the most labor-intensive sectors within agriculture. Large dairies can employ more than 30 people to feed, monitor, and milk the herd up to three times a day.[8] The labor-intensive nature of dairies led to the first automated milking system (AMS) in 1992. Since then, the technology has advanced.

In the 2020s, AMS allows the cows to decide when they want to be milked. Each cow is fitted with an electronic tracker. When a cow walks into a stall, the robotic milker identifies the cow via the tracker. The robot uses a laser-guided system to wash the cow's udders and attach the milking cups. Data on the quality and quantity of the cow's milk is collected and analyzed as the cow enjoys a snack while being milked.

Production of fruits and vegetables is also labor-intensive, especially at harvest. Robots with cameras and AI capabilities can now sense if fruits or vegetables are ripe and then carefully collect them. Other robots are being trained to work autonomously to haul ripe produce from the field and deliver it to collection points.

Immigrants are a large part of the agricultural workforce. From 2019 to 2020, nearly 70 percent of all farm workers were foreign-born, and they earned less than $14 per hour on average.[9] American farms need about 2.4 million temporary workers each year, yet those workers are becoming hard to find due to low wages and difficult conditions such as extreme heat.[10] Farmers have little control over the prices they receive for their products, so it can be difficult for them to offer higher wages.

Robots can also help weed fields. Robots armed with cameras can detect and treat weeds as they find them. Some use a robotic hoe, while other models use a lightning-like strike or fire to kill weeds without using herbicides. The robot uses metal rods to shoot a jolt of electricity onto the weeds. Other in-field robots work like vacuums to suck up unwanted pests, avoiding the use of insecticides.

A robotic feed pusher helps ensure livestock get the nutrition they need to grow and stay healthy.

AI AND MACHINE LEARNING

Autonomous vehicles and robots rely on AI and machine learning to operate smoothly. AI also is helping farmers make decisions on the farm. At the beginning of the year, AI can analyze historical and real-time soil temperature and moisture data to predict the best times to plant crops based on seeds and growing conditions. As crop plants emerge and begin to grow, AI can help farmers identify emerging crop diseases and insect challenges using digital photos snapped with

Robots are currently much more expensive than human workers for jobs such as picking strawberries, but costs are likely to come down over time.

a smartphone. This information can be mapped and fed into equipment that uses VRT to apply fertilizer and pesticides only where needed.

Farm economics plays a role in how quickly robotics and new technology are accepted. A robotic strawberry-picking system can cost $250,000.[11] Picking strawberries by hand can cost more than $6,500 per acre.[12] The costs of these options, along with the efficiency of each method, will determine whether farmers switch to automated techniques.

If automation is the solution, it also means new skilled labor will be needed to operate the robotic systems. Such workers may be difficult to find in more remote rural areas. If robotic systems experience problems, it may also be hard to find technicians to troubleshoot and repair them.

CHAPTER FIVE

GROWING AND PROTECTING CROPS

Innovations in hybridization, seed genetics, and GMOs powered the dramatic crop yield increases of the 1900s and early 2000s. Yet today's higher-yielding crops still require protection from pests, diseases, and environmental conditions that threaten to sicken or destroy them. Natural and synthetic fertilizers, chemical pesticides, and beneficial microorganisms are some of the tools modern farmers use to protect the yield potential of their crops.

Synthetic fertilizers are a common source of crop nutrients on modern farms, especially farms that don't raise livestock. Synthetic fertilizers became popular during the green revolution because of their wide availability and their ability to increase plant growth. Before synthetic fertilizers, farmers fertilized their crops with organic materials,

Fertilizers add crucial nutrients such as potassium, phosphorus, and nitrogen to the soil.

including animal manure, bones, fish waste, wood ashes, and other by-products. Organic fertilizers are still used today.

Both synthetic and organic fertilizers can interact with microbes in the soil to emit nitrous oxide, a greenhouse gas that contributes to climate change. In addition, both synthetic and organic fertilizers can leach, or move off, fields and into waterways, where they can lead to dangerous levels of pollutants. Many modern farmers are rethinking the way they apply these nutrients to help prevent this pollution.

In addition to using less fertilizer and using fertilizer only where needed, many farmers have changed the timing of fertilizer use. Historically, fertilizers were often applied in the fall after harvesting because snowmelt and rain could wash away nutrients in the winter and spring. Research indicated that applying fertilizers in season is safer than applying them in the fall, when they are more likely to leach into water or volatilize as dangerous ammonia. More farmers are shifting to applying fertilizer only at planting or as crops grow.

Other farmers have started to use nitrogen stabilizers. These stabilizers prevent plant nutrients from leaching or volatilizing. They also prevent nutrients from converting into forms that can be more easily leached or volatilized. Applying fertilizer using drip irrigation or other high-efficiency irrigation systems can also make it easier for crops to take in and use nutrients.

The use of controlled-release fertilizers is another solution that is becoming more popular. These products feature nutrients covered in coatings that break down over time. This controls the amount, availability, and timing of nutrient release. Controlled-release fertilizers can be applied

Farmers worldwide use more than 3.8 million short tons (3.4 million metric tons) of pesticides on crops each year.

just once in a growing season and provide nutrients through the full life cycle of the plant.

PESTICIDES

Pesticides are products that protect crops from weeds, insects, and diseases that can affect crop yields. They include herbicides, which target harmful plants; insecticides, which target harmful insects; and fungicides, which target harmful fungi. Pesticides have improved since early farmers first used commonly available chemicals, including arsenic and sulfur.

Modern pesticides are more likely to directly target a group of pests and be less toxic to farm workers. The active ingredients in modern pesticides may be bred directly into the plant with genetic modification, applied to the seed as a treatment, or applied over the top of crops. Farmers can use technology to target pesticides only in areas where they are needed.

Unlike earlier pesticides, the next generation of pesticides is more likely to tap into nature's own plant defense mechanisms. For example, the chrysanthemum and the bottle brush plant produce their own compounds that fend off insects and weeds, respectively. Chemicals found in chrysanthemums are used in a class of synthetic insecticides, and a chemical in bottle brush plants is a popular compound in a class of synthetic herbicides. One of the newest classes of synthetic insecticides uses a protein found in spider venom.

THE FARM CREDIT SYSTEM

Farmers must buy inputs for their crops long before they sell those crops. In 2024, corn inputs averaged more than $500 per acre, and those for soybeans more than $250 per acre.[2] Affording these inputs early in the growing season can be difficult. This is why the US government created the Farm Credit System in 1916. Today, Farm Credit continues to provide loans to farmers and other rural businesses. Farmers may take out operating loans for the next season's crop or loans for other business purchases, including farmland, buildings such as sheds or grain bins, or equipment.

Farmers work to match available pesticides with the specific problems they are facing in the field. Some herbicides are designed to prevent weeds from sprouting, while others are designed to kill weeds once they are actively competing with the crop. Fungicides can be applied when disease strikes or when forecasting tools identify conditions for an outbreak, such as when rain is expected or humidity is high. Insecticides can be tailored to the stage of development of a particular insect. Some products may kill insect larvae, while others control adult pests.

When one type of pesticide is used often, a small portion of the targeted insects or weeds may survive due to their unique genetic makeup. When these resistant insects or weeds reproduce, the new generation has these traits, too, making them resistant to the pesticide. Often pesticides are combined and applied together because different products are effective at handling different species of pests. Using a combination of pesticides helps prevent the development of resistant weeds, insects, and diseases.

Despite these efforts, pesticide-resistant diseases, weeds, and insects are on the rise around the world, while climate change is threatening to make pest control even harder. For example, rising temperatures allow insects to digest faster, meaning they eat more. Insects are more active and reproduce at a quicker rate in warmer temperatures. In response, modern pesticide manufacturers are using AI to research new pesticide compounds designed to address resistance and climate change.

ORGANIC FARMING

Organic farming is growing crops and raising animals without the use of synthetic fertilizers or pesticides or genetic modification. The USDA began its organic certification program in 2002. Organic farms have grown steadily since that time, and in 2022 about five million acres (2 million ha) of US land were organic certified. While the organic movement originally focused on pastures and rangeland, organic farmers now produce a wide variety of products. Roughly 3 percent of sales by US farms are organic, even though organic farming

Organic produce costs more than standard produce. Still, the popularity of organic food has risen steadily since the early 2000s.

happens on less than 1 percent of all farmland.[3]

While organic production offers farmers higher margins for their products, the transition to an organic system takes three years, during which any production from the farm cannot be sold as organic. Transitioning farmers must deal with the reduced yields from an organic production system during this time without being able to charge the higher price of organic foods. Despite this barrier, an increasing number of farmers are choosing organic production systems to increase long-term farm income. The USDA has jumped in as well, with new programs to aid farmers in the transition to organic production.

Organic farming relies on pesticide methods that were used before synthetic pesticides were developed. Many of these products require higher application rates than synthetic pesticides. Organic production also can involve more tilling than conventional or regenerative systems. This is because organic weed control options are more limited. Growing interest in organics has spurred more research and development in seed genetics. Organic producers hope this will lead to plants with higher yields that are naturally more resistant to pests.

BIOLOGICALS

On modern farms, synthetic fertilizers and pesticides continue to be most effective. Yet a growing number of firms are developing new products based on natural materials or processes. These new products are known as biologicals, and they are made from microorganisms, beneficial insects, or plant extracts.

There are three main types of biologicals. Biostimulants boost a crop's natural processes in order to improve plant growth and health. Biofertilizers help plants take in nutrients more efficiently. And biopesticides control insects, diseases, and weeds.

Nematodes are a major pest problem around the world. These microscopic, wormlike pests feed on crop roots.

Bee vectoring takes advantage of natural bee behaviors to precisely apply biologicals to plants.

One popular biological seed treatment for soybeans features a naturally occurring parasite of the nematode that attacks and kills it. Delivering the parasite directly into the soil on the planted seed places the pest-controlling agent where it's needed most. Other biological products use naturally occurring beneficial soil fungi and bacteria. These bacteria can work symbiotically with plants, feeding off fluids shed by a plant's roots while protecting the plant from pests and diseases. These products can be applied to seeds or directly to soil at the time of planting.

Scientists have found unique ways to apply biological control agents to plants. These agents are living organisms that can be used to control pests. Using ladybugs to control an aphid infestation is one example. Bee vectoring uses pollinating bees to apply biological products directly to the flowers of specialty crops such as strawberries, apples, and tomatoes. The biological control agents are placed in special trays within the beehive. Bees pick up the control agents when they leave the hive and deposit them on the target crops as a part of the natural pollination process.

Climate change is boosting farmers' interest in biologicals, especially those that can help plants better withstand increased heat, drought, and other forms of stress. These biostimulants are becoming an add-on to traditional fertilizer and pesticide programs. Using multiple tools in this way has proven to boost yields, reduce the use of chemical pesticides, and help prevent development of resistance. Biological products do have some drawbacks. Since they use living organisms, they require special storage and handling, which may not be feasible for all farmers.

ANIMAL AGRICULTURE

The average American eats more than 200 pounds (91 kg) of meat per year.[1] As standards of living rise around the world, other consumers are eager to add more meat and dairy to their diets too. Modern animal agriculture production is faced with supplying this growing demand while also addressing societal demands for sustainability and animal welfare. New and evolving technologies are stepping up to meet these challenges by changing how animals on farms are selected, monitored, fed, and cared for.

These changes come with costs. The average cost of a single robotic milking machine can exceed $150,000.[2] This technology is more feasible for large operations that can spread the costs over a bigger herd of animals. Adopting the technology also means fewer workers are needed to handle the

Advanced equipment such as robotic milking machines can require enormous up-front costs, putting them out of reach for small farms.

same number of animals. This means large operations have an advantage over smaller operations, which carry higher production costs and can't compete. The dairy industry is an example of how economies of scale influence production efficiency. In 1987, half of all dairy farms had herds of 80 or fewer cows. By 2017, half had herds of 1,300 or fewer cows.[3]

James MacDonald is an agricultural researcher at the University of Maryland. In 2023 he said, "Consolidation in dairy is just dramatic, with shifts to much bigger farms and smaller farms going out of business. The last two years, 15 percent of the dairy farms in the country went out of business."[4] New technologies during this period allowed larger dairy operators to handle more cows. Yet paying for these technologies required higher volumes of milk sales.

Roughly half of modern farming operations include livestock.[5] Cattle are the most widely produced species, accounting for about one-third of all money made from farm livestock sales in 2022. Poultry and eggs are next, with nearly 30 percent of sales. Dairy cows accounted for 22 percent of sales, and pigs are at about 12 percent.[6]

Livestock play multiple roles on the world's farms. In developing nations, farmers still rely on livestock to feed their own families in addition to providing income. Animal manure supplies fertilizer for crops when synthetic options are unavailable or too costly. And ruminants such as cattle, goats, and sheep are able to process nutrients from grasses, leaves, and other plant material that humans can't eat. Roughly two-thirds of agricultural land around the world is unsuitable for growing crops, but grazing animals can use this land and add to the global food supply.[7]

BETTER GENETICS

Selective breeding and gene editing technologies are creating more productive farm animals in the same way

Researchers preserve genetic material from livestock in ultra-cold containers.

they are creating higher-yielding crops. Dairy farmers were among the first to use selective breeding to improve the quantity and quality of milk from their herds. Beginning in the 1940s, dairy farmers could use artificial insemination to breed their cows with semen from dairy bulls known to produce high-performing offspring. Artificial insemination rapidly became the standard in the dairy industry, and the genetics databases that followed enabled producers to create high-performing genetic matchups. Modern dairy cows produce roughly four times more milk than they did in the mid-1900s.[9]

Current technology also allows for sex selection in livestock. This increases the chances of having a female calf that can produce milk, rather than a male calf, which is less valuable. Scientists have also used genetic engineering to give more cattle breeds a short, slick coat suited for hot weather.

Beef cattle, poultry, and swine genetics also have benefited from selective breeding, artificial insemination, and new genotyping technology. Early work in genetics identified animals that produced the leaner cuts of meat consumers demanded. Producers now can select breeding animals by how efficiently they transform feed into weight gain and how large and healthy their offspring tend to be.

The future of animal genetics promises continued improvements in these production areas and new opportunities in disease prevention. Gene editing is being used in swine genetics to develop pigs that are naturally resistant to porcine reproductive and respiratory syndrome (PRRS) virus. PRRS is a major global disease that is responsible for the death of roughly 20 percent of the global swine herd each year.[10] Gene editing also is targeting *Salmonella*, a pathogen in poultry that can make people sick.

ANIMAL WELFARE TECHNOLOGIES

Keeping barns and pens clean and comfortable is a time-consuming job that pays off in healthier, happier animals. With operations becoming larger and available workers fewer, some farmers are turning to technology to help. Livestock producers now have access to automated cleaning systems that can work around the clock to move manure from barns to a central collection area. Automated bedding systems apply fresh bedding, such as straw, sawdust, or wood shavings, to pen areas several times per day. Some barns even include a sensor-equipped brush that begins spinning when an animal touches it to scratch an itch and stops automatically when the animal walks away.

Farms are also adding environmental sensors and control systems to barns. This technology provides real-time data on

An automated slat pusher cleans a cow barn in Germany by sliding manure through slots on the floor.

conditions and makes adjustments to help animals grow and keep them comfortable. Systems can monitor barns for air and water quality and pollutants, along with levels of noise, light, heat, and humidity. One study found that improved heating systems in piglet environments reduced not only energy usage but also piglet deaths.

Audio analysis and imaging are other technologies anticipated to improve animal welfare and productivity. Pork producers have always struggled with losing piglets when their mothers inadvertently crush them. A new system in piglet nurseries attaches a wearable device to the mother pig, or sow, and monitors for the sound of a piglet

Farmers in Japan are using sensors on cattle that can track the herd's activity level over time. This can help them spot early signs of illness.

being crushed. Upon identifying the sound, the wearable uses gentle electrical signals to let the sow know to move and release the piglet.

Poultry producers also have a new tool to identify the destructive pecking that has long been a hallmark of poultry flocks. Intelligent camera systems can detect pecking and other dangerous behaviors in flocks. This allows producers to identify and isolate problematic animals without having to constantly monitor the poultry facility.

Enhanced monitoring and thermal imaging are proving to be helpful tools in quickly identifying and rapidly treating health conditions. New systems can record the sounds of pigs coughing to determine if animals are becoming ill before the disease spreads to the rest of the herd. Poultry producers can get alerts on their smartphones if AI-paired cameras detect birds moving differently than normal, which can be an early indicator of disease.

Thermal imaging can be used to detect conditions such as lameness in cattle. Lameness and other injuries and inflammation cause parts of the body to become hotter than usual, and thermal cameras can see this heat. Farmers can then isolate and treat the animal. Thermal imagery in milking systems can also be used to detect mastitis, a painful and contagious inflammation of the mammary gland.

FEED INNOVATIONS

Data systems, analytics, and sensors are transforming the way US livestock are fed and cared for. Modern farmers have far more information on the content, quality, consumption, and nutritional impact of animal feed than at any time in the past. Data is taking the guesswork out of creating feed rations for animals to achieve specific weight and health outcomes.

The main ingredients of modern animal feeds are corn, soybean meal, and distillers' dried grains and solubles (DDGS), a by-product of ethanol production. To these building blocks, animal nutritionists mix in a tailored collection of additives designed to optimize animal growth and health. These additives include vitamins, probiotics, enzymes, minerals, and amino acids. Probiotics are live bacteria that can have health benefits when consumed. Nutritionists must understand how each of these feed ingredients affects particular species at specific times in their life cycles. Failure to account for how well the feed is digested and the efficiency with which nutrients are absorbed can lead to poor performance and health.

Feed and related innovations are being used to reduce the use of antibiotics in livestock. Researchers are developing antimicrobial probiotics that can kill harmful bacteria or viruses in livestock before they get sick. In dairy cattle, a new product uses sound waves to stimulate a cow's natural disease-fighting response to treat mastitis, which historically was treated with antibiotics.

Feeding systems are evolving to support more customized nutrition programs as well. In swine, cameras with machine learning software can recognize individual pigs, avoiding the need for tags and enabling customized feeding and veterinary care. Dairy calves can suckle from a computerized system instead of a mother cow, with data on their intake going to farmers' smartphones for monitoring.

Multiple species are being fitted with the animal equivalent of a fitness tracker to monitor movement, health, and feed intake. Robotic milking systems track the performance of individual cows. Technology is also advancing farming methods beyond the dairy barn. New growing methods in controlled environments are improving plant health and increasing harvests.

CLEANER COW BURPS

Methane is a greenhouse gas that is even more effective than carbon dioxide at trapping heat in the atmosphere. Roughly 30 percent of the world's human-caused methane emissions come from ruminant animals raised for meat and milk.[11] Methane is created as part of the natural digestion process and then emitted primarily through burping.

Researchers developed a feed additive that helps prevent the formation of methane in ruminants' stomachs. Studies done on the feed additive found that it reduces methane burps from dairy cows by an average of 30 percent and from beef cows by an average of 45 percent.[12]

CHAPTER SEVEN

CEA SYSTEMS

Controlled environment agriculture (CEA) systems are among the many technologies that are changing the face of modern farming. CEA systems grow plants in enclosed spaces where factors such as temperature, humidity, light, and nutrients can be controlled to produce optimal growing conditions. The ability to create a perfect plant environment has been linked to increased quality and yield, with some greenhouse operators reporting a 30-fold yield increase per acre.[1] CEA systems include indoor hydroponic systems, greenhouses, aquaponics, and aeroponic vertical farms.

CEA systems are becoming more popular as a changing climate makes open-field growing conditions less predictable. In addition, these systems are being promoted as a way to bring food

Setting up CEA systems is expensive, but having precise
control over crops can greatly boost productivity.

production closer to urban areas that lack the large areas of land necessary for open-field farming. Building a CEA system near or within an urban area, such as on a rooftop, can lower the costs and environmental impact of food by reducing the need to transport it from faraway farms.

CEA systems improve crop production and soil management as well. Some farmers prefer CEA systems for their ability to create specific conditions that enable their crop to grow as quickly and as efficiently as possible. A CEA system can enable year-round food production in climates that may be too hot or too cold at least part of each year while also protecting against crop damage from storms or flooding. Closed systems also can help avoid infestations of natural pests, such as insects, and reduce the chance for the introduction of potential contaminants, including germs that can cause foodborne illnesses such as *E. coli* or *Salmonella*.

GREENHOUSES

Greenhouses have been used since ancient Rome to harness the sun's light and warmth to extend the growing season. Modern greenhouses come in many shapes, from small temporary structures with plastic sheeting over a tunnel of high hoops to high-tech permanent installations that cover many acres of land. The traditional glass panes of greenhouses have given way to sturdier plastics. Many modern greenhouses feature energy-efficient LED lighting systems to extend light hours as necessary. Greenhouses offer flexible growing environments, whether located in rural areas or perched atop roofs in cities.

Climate control is a critical element in modern CEA greenhouses. Heating and cooling systems, along with vents and fans, allow growers to maintain specific conditions. These tools can be customized to both the crop being grown and the environment outside the greenhouse. For example, greenhouses in cold climates may have

Companies in the United Arab Emirates, a desert nation where outdoor farming is challenging, have experimented with indoor vertical farms.

drapes that help keep the cold air out. Popular food crops

for greenhouse production include tomatoes, peppers,

and cucumbers.

VERTICAL FARMS

Like greenhouses, vertical farms have been a part of

agriculture for centuries. The Hanging Gardens of Babylon,

said to have been built in the 600s or 500s BCE, are

considered the first vertical farm. The gardens are described in many ancient texts, though their true location has not

been determined. Their stacked terraces and basic irrigation

system are the ancestors of today's high-tech vertical farms,

which feature stacked layers or shelves of crops. Unlike the

Babylonian gardens, modern vertical farms rely on artificial

light and soil-less growing systems.

Vertical farms offer several advantages over even

high-tech greenhouses. Stacked production systems and

precise growing conditions

can create crop yields that

are 10 to 20 times higher

than the yields of those crops

in conventional farming

systems.[4] With no need for

windows or glass panes,

vertical farms can be set up

in shipping containers or

old warehouses, offering

new uses for what might

otherwise be wasted space.

Since 2022, strawberries

have become a popular vertical farming crop. Sam Bertram

is the CEO of OnePointOne, a vertical farming company that

SOLAR FARMS

Some farmers are earning income by hosting solar arrays on their land. Combining solar power generation with agricultural production is called agrivoltaics. This term is a blend of the words *agriculture* and *photovoltaics*, the technology used in solar panels. The US National Renewable Energy Laboratory reported more than 300 agrivoltaic projects across the United States in 2023.[5] The nation's largest agrivoltaic site is at a blueberry farm in Maine.

grows strawberries in Arizona. He explains that the ability to control the environment allows farmers to grow many different varieties. "There are thousands of different cultivars of strawberry that you can find, but when you're talking about the grocery store there are three or four," Bertram says.[6] This limited selection is because only a few types grow well in outdoor fields. Vertical farming could make a wider variety of strawberries available to consumers.

Vertical farms are reliant on artificial lighting and climate control technology. These systems are primarily designed to produce leafy greens, herbs, and other similar lightweight, fast-growing produce. Like high-tech greenhouses, vertical farming systems make efficient use of water and nutrients.

A key drawback of vertical farms is their energy requirements. Without nature's free sunlight and water, all inputs must be provided artificially. Regulating humidity also can require significant investments in heating, ventilation, and air-conditioning systems. Electricity usage per pound of produce within a vertical farm growing leafy greens is estimated to be 75 times that of greens production in a field. For small fruits such as strawberries, vertical farm production requires an estimated 120 times the electricity of in-field production per pound of berries.[7]

HYDROPONIC AND AEROPONIC SYSTEMS

Both high-tech greenhouses and vertical farms can make use of soil-less production systems. Plant scientists began growing plants without soil more than 100 years ago for research purposes. High-tech greenhouses or vertical farms may use hydroponic systems. These systems involve planting seeds in a nutrient solution or a non-soil-based substrate, such as ground coconut husks or peat moss. Aeroponics, where plant roots are exposed to air and regularly misted with nutrient-rich water, is another option in some CEA systems.

Both hydroponic and aeroponic systems deliver nutrients to plants through water-based solutions.

Adapting row-crop staples such as wheat to controlled growing environments could help produce sufficient food supplies in the future as climate change threatens to disrupt conventional farming. To test this possibility, researchers used a crop simulation tool to predict wheat yields in a 10-floor vertical farm covering less than 2.5 acres (1 ha). The tool predicted that optimal conditions in a CEA system would increase wheat yield by 600 times compared with the global average, while using significantly less land.[8] However, the energy required to run such a farm could be cost-prohibitive and potentially harmful to the environment, depending on the energy source.

Aeroponic farmers can carefully tune the amount and type of light their plants receive.

Because nutrients are given directly to the plants, the plants in these systems do not have to create extensive root systems to access nutrients. This allows hydroponic and aeroponic systems to support more plants per square foot than traditional soil-based farming, with higher yields. For example, high-tech greenhouses have produced a pepper yield that is 10 times the weight of open-field production per acre.[9]

Hydroponic and aeroponic systems also use water more efficiently than open-field production. Water from hydroponic systems can deliver nutrients in a more precise manner, and the water can be recycled after use by the crop. Reduction in water use can top 85 percent in high-tech greenhouses and even 90 percent in vertical farms compared with open-field production of the same crops.[10]

AQUACULTURE AND AQUAPONICS

Hydroponics and aeroponics systems produce food from plants. Two other CEA systems can produce fish and shellfish along with plants. Aquaculture is the production of underwater plants, fish, and shellfish in either fresh or salt water. Aquaponics combines aquaculture with plant production in the absence of soil. Aquaponics uses waste from the fish to feed plants, which filter out the waste for use in water recirculation systems.

Aquaculture in contained systems with continuous water reuse has been in place since the early 1980s. Prior to that, most aquaculture took place in outdoor environments. While CEA aquaculture systems are more costly to build and operate than their outdoor counterparts, they offer several unique benefits. Closed systems can prevent farmed species from escaping into the wild. These systems deliver more consistent water temperatures, which can facilitate fish growth. In addition, more fish can be produced in less space than with pond-based aquaculture systems.

Aquaponics grew out of the challenge of managing waste in aquaculture systems. The first closed-loop aquaponic system was developed in the mid-1980s and featured drip irrigation of water from fish tanks to nourish tomatoes and cucumbers in sand grow beds. The plants thrived on the waste while also filtering the tank water, cleaning it for recirculation back into the fish tanks.

Modern aquaponics systems continue to build on the concept. Superior Fresh operates the world's largest aquaponic farm in central Wisconsin. The farm produces nearly 1.5 million pounds (680,000 kg) of salmon and more than three million pounds (1.4 million kg) of leafy greens each year. Steve Summerfelt is lead scientist at Superior Fresh. He says, "Our salmon is fed organic-certified feed and is certified non-GMO by A Greener World, with a 'heartcheck healthy' certification from the American Heart Association."[11] The self-contained system operates year-round despite Wisconsin's cold winters, bringing fresh fish and produce to areas that might otherwise have to transport those foods from distant fields and ponds.

But CEA systems cannot be used to grow all crops. They are not suited for producing the nation's largest crops, which are row crops such as corn, wheat, and soybeans.

CEA systems also are expensive to build and run. One of the largest CEA systems in the United States is a 20-acre (8 ha) hydroponic greenhouse in central Texas.[12] The facility grows a variety of lettuces and promises to deliver produce within 24 to 48 hours of harvest. Greenhouse owners reported that the facility cost around $150 million to build and requires roughly 120 employees.[13]

Despite these challenges, innovation in CEA systems continues as farmers around the world seek new ways to meet consumer demand for more local food while using land and water resources more efficiently. Existing geographic limitations to food production, combined with a growing population and climate change challenges, will only add to these needs.

CHAPTER EIGHT

REGENERATIVE AGRICULTURE

Rising concerns about climate change, soil and water degradation, and input costs are leading some farmers to revisit older farm management practices. These practices include less tilling or disturbance of the soil, integrating livestock with growing crops, avoiding bare soil, rotating multiple crops across fields and growing seasons, and maintaining living roots in the soil year-round. These practices are commonly referred to as regenerative agriculture.

Regenerative agriculture focuses on improving the quality of the soil to help it function more efficiently and effectively. Soil performs many jobs for farmers. It provides a home and food for plants and animals, including microscopic organisms such as bacteria and fungi. Soil also plays a critical role in managing water. Healthy soils rapidly absorb water

Regenerative agriculture is all about promoting sustainability in modern farming.

and help filter it. Degraded soils may lack the structure to effectively manage water, leading to flooding and runoff.

Healthy soils also store more carbon. Soils are made of a mix of minerals, air, water, and organic matter, which can be either living or dead organisms. Under certain conditions, a portion of the organic matter becomes soil organic carbon. Storing, or sequestering, carbon in the soil keeps it from entering the atmosphere, where it would add to the problem of climate change.

Many regenerative farming practices have been around for hundreds of years. Farmers moved away from these practices as new tools and methods became available, such as synthetic fertilizer and tillage capabilities. Farmers shifted away from using traditional techniques because these new technologies and methods increased yields. Today, regenerative agriculture is bringing back these traditional methods and combining them with new tools and technologies.

REDUCED SOIL DISTURBANCE

Limiting how often and how much soil is disturbed is a key part of regenerative agriculture. This means replacing tillage, the use of machines such as tractors to turn soils and prepare them for planting, with alternative technologies. Regenerative farmers are now using advanced no-tillage equipment and modern herbicides.

Traditional plowing tools, such as moldboard plows, sliced and turned over soil at depths of up to a foot (0.3 m).[2] This created a weed-free, receptive bed for planting seeds, but it left the soil exposed to erosion by wind and water. It also damaged the structure of the soil, making it less able to hold water.

Advanced tillage equipment can strip-till, which disturbs only the soil in the crop row. This equipment

FARM SKILLS FOR ALL

Students with an interest in agriculture but no access to a farm can still get engaged in the industry by participating in 4-H or FFA. 4-H is a club-based national youth organization. Local 4-H clubs offer hands-on skill development in a range of areas, including agriculture. FFA is a national nonprofit career and technical student organization that offers agricultural training for students in middle and high schools around the country, including in some urban areas. These organizations are helping train the next generation of farmers.

No-till farming methods benefit from leaving residue from past growing seasons on the field.

can also ridge-till, which builds and moves soil on a raised bed for planting. Both of these methods allow farmers to leave crop residue in the field. This is the waste material left behind after a field has been harvested. It helps protect the soil from erosion while retaining its organic matter content, which improves the health of the soil.

No-till systems allow farmers to skip tillage altogether and avoid the associated fuel costs. No-till planting equipment is designed to cut a single narrow furrow through the undisturbed soil and crop residue from the prior year, place the seed, and cover it, all in one pass. Special additions to planters, called row cleaners, help push residue from earlier crops and larger clumps of uneven soil to the side to help the planter function more effectively.

Farmers in no-till systems have several options for controlling weeds as well. Modern herbicides can quickly and effectively kill weeds. Crops can be rotated to reduce the likelihood of a particular weed species becoming dominant or harder to control. Planting a cover crop in between plantings of commercial crops can crowd out weeds before they have a chance to grow. Avoiding soil disturbance also prevents the unintentional spreading of weed seeds that may already be in the soil.

LIVING ROOTS

Maintaining a living root in the soil all year is another key principle of regenerative agriculture. In annual cropping systems, these living roots are called cover crops. Cover crops are not typically harvested like a commercial crop. Instead, they provide benefits both below and above ground that contribute over time to more successful growth of the commercial crop.

Living plants take in sunlight and carbon dioxide and transfer carbon to the soil via their roots. This benefit goes away after harvest of a commercial crop in conventional cropping systems. In regenerative systems, root growth from cover crops continues to help aerate the soil and improve its structure for better water cycling and plant growth. Cover crop roots also hold nutrients in the soil that commercial crops can later use. Using different species of cover crops allows farmers to manage the amount of nutrients available for commercial crops as well.

Above ground, cover crops create a protective blanket over the soil, reducing erosion by wind and water. Cover crops can help moderate soil temperatures and reduce compaction of the soil from heavy rains. Wildlife and grazing animals can benefit from cover crops as a food source.

Rye is commonly used as a cover crop. Its deep roots help hold the soil in place.

Wildlife also can use cover crops for habitat. Cover crops can help reduce weeds and provide added biodiversity. This has been shown to reduce pests and add more nutrients.

COVER CROP ADVANCES

Cover crops are not without challenges, however. Farmers in northern growing environments may struggle to grow cover crops between harvest and the onset of winter weather. New interseeding tools allow farmers to plant cover crops while the commercial crop is still in the field. These tools include using aerial seeding or drop tubes mounted on high-boy tractors designed to travel above crops in the field. Herbicides may be needed to kill cover crops before spring planting. Cover crops also can be crushed with a roller crimper, which works much like a road roller.

The growing popularity of cover crops is leading to more investment in cover-crop genetics, planting systems, and management. Researchers are working to develop cover crop seeds light enough to be applied by drones. AI is being developed to answer common farmer questions on cover crops and no-till methods. Data analytics is also being used to cross-reference soil carbon testing results with the regenerative management practices that created them.

Data analytics also can help farmers move from a single species of cover crop to a sophisticated blend of seeds designed for specific outcomes. Rick Clark, a regenerative farmer in Indiana, swears by this method. "I'm going to put out as many things as I possibly can in that cocktail for diversification." he says. "We can fall into a trap of a monoculture in cover crops just like we can fall into a trap of monoculture in cash crops."[3] Some farmers are employing blends of nearly a dozen different seeds to address variable weather, soil, nutrient, and crop rotation situations.

LIVESTOCK AND REGENERATIVE FARMING

Animal agriculture has become a key part of regenerative farming as well. Livestock allowed on fields graze on cover crops, which supplements the feed they usually eat. Grazing livestock also add nutrients to the fields through their manure, potentially reducing the need for synthetic nutrients later in the crop cycle.

Short-duration, high-intensity grazing is another regenerative technique farmers are using to improve soil and plant health in pastures and rangeland. The technique, also known as mob grazing, limits animals to a small patch of land for a limited time. Animals graze down the land before being moved to a different place. The technique allows for longer recovery times for grazed areas and encourages animals to eat a more diverse diet of available feed.

Mob grazing is getting help from technology as well. GPS-enabled collars can be placed on grazing animals to create a virtual fence. Changing the location of the fence is as easy as making a few taps using an app on a smartphone.

If an animal wanders too close to the virtual fence, the collar makes a musical sound. If the animal keeps going, it gets a small electric shock. A livestock farmer in Scotland explained that it took about a week to train the cows to stay within the designated area without getting shocked. Farmers can also use the app to track the location of livestock, which helps alert them to possible problems.

CARBON FARMING

The ability of regenerative farming practices to sequester carbon in soil has created an opportunity for farmers to make additional money. Through the voluntary carbon market, farmers get paid for carbon they remove from the atmosphere and store in their soil for a certain amount of time. This carbon, called carbon assets, is purchased by companies seeking to offset, or cancel out, greenhouse gas emissions from their businesses. Different farming operations can sequester varying amounts of carbon depending on local soils, crops grown, environmental conditions, and their farm management practices.

Carbon farming requires farmers to maintain detailed records of their farming practices as a means of verifying the stored carbon. Carbon sequestration also can be

RICK CLARK

Rick Clark grew up in Williamsport, Indiana, on a farm that has been in his family since the 1880s. He left the farm to earn a degree in agriculture and economics at Purdue University, followed by four years in Chicago, Illinois, where he traded bonds on the Chicago Stock Exchange. Eventually, Clark ended up back on the farm, with a new appreciation for the business of farming.

In the mid-2010s, Danone, an international food company Clark grew crops for, asked if he could supply GMO-free grain. The request pushed Clark to reconsider his approach to farming. "It made me start thinking differently about how I was doing things and how I could pivot to meet consumer demand."[5] Clark decided to use a regenerative farming approach to grow non-GMO seeds.

He stopped focusing on yield and began to think about soil health and diversity. He rotated his crops regularly, planted cover crops, and turned to no-till farming methods. In the years since, the farm has been very profitable. Clark is slowly transitioning acreage to organic. And he's teaching other farmers how to make the shift to regenerative farming as well.

REGENERATIVE FOOD

Many food companies are embracing regenerative agriculture due to its ability to reduce greenhouse gas emissions and remove carbon. Companies including Pepsi, General Mills, Nestlé, and Land O'Lakes have made commitments to work toward more regenerative practices within their supply chains. These companies are working with farmers and others in the food system to track production practices on fields that supply widely used crops such as corn and wheat. This information is used to measure emissions and report on progress companies have made on publicly stated commitments to more sustainable food products.

verified by regular soil tests to measure soil organic carbon. Computer modeling programs are used to calculate likely soil organic carbon levels based on crops, farming practices, soil types, and other factors.

Carbon farming is being promoted as an exciting new opportunity for farmers to make additional income. Farmer participation in such programs has been limited, however, due to the challenges of adopting regenerative farming practices. Farming remains an inherently risky business, with factors including weather and markets operating well beyond the control of the farmer. Any change to a farming practice or a crop input can be a source of risk, even practices such as adopting cover crops that have been shown to offer significant long-term benefits.

These risks have focused attention on the need for other participants in the food industry to share some of the risks of adopting new practices. Some large food companies have made commitments to support farmers who adopt regenerative agriculture practices. These companies have realized that these practices can result in a more reliable and resilient food system. In turn, the companies are able to keep their own commitments to help mitigate climate change.

By combining practices that are good for the environment with technological advances, modern farmers have the ability to efficiently produce more food for a growing population. Precision planting technology paired with GPS gives farmers the ability to adjust applications of water, fertilizer, and other inputs to address a crop's specific needs. The automation of daily tasks such as milking a dairy herd and monitoring livestock in the field can now be done with an app. And drones provide a bird's-eye view of crops in a fraction of the time it would take to walk the fields.

Issues such as climate change will continue to challenge farmers. But modern farmers are equipped with high-tech tools, along with innovative techniques for solving problems in a way that benefits everyone. These advancements will help agriculture continue to adapt in the future.

FARMING TODAY

- Modern farms are larger, less numerous, and more productive than at any other time in human history.

- The United States is home to fewer than two million farms, with each farmer feeding an average of 166 people in the United States and abroad each year.

NEW TECHNOLOGY

- Genetically modified seeds, next-generation pesticides, and farm vehicles that steer themselves using GPS technology represent the largest categories of technology adoption on farms.

- Drones are growing in popularity among businesses that serve farmers, including crop consultants and agricultural retailers.

- Ongoing labor shortages in rural areas are making automation more attractive despite its high cost. Automated systems often can feed production and performance data directly into farm management systems.

AGRICULTURE AND THE ENVIRONMENT

- Unpredictable weather and a rise in consumer interest in the food system has increased investment in controlled growing environments such as vertical farms. These systems have higher production costs than open-field agriculture.

- Synthetic fertilizers and heavy tillage equipment, combined with larger farms staffed by fewer workers, spurred widespread growth in input-intensive agriculture. This had the unintended effect of increasing soil erosion and reducing soil quality on many fields.

- Regenerative agriculture focuses on building healthier, better-functioning soils by disturbing soil less, planting cover crops, rotating crops, and integrating animal agriculture.

QUOTE

"Working with technology partners and trading partners . . . helps us realize the benefits of our sustainability efforts up and down the supply chain. By allowing sustainability information to flow with the supply chain, downstream producers can help show what they are doing on the farm to make a better environment and world."

—*Lukas Fricke, farmer*

GLOSSARY

artificial insemination
The breeding of livestock via a medical procedure using semen based on the preferred genetics for the offspring.

artificial intelligence (AI)
Computer systems that can learn, write, analyze, and perform other tasks associated with human intelligence.

autonomous
Capable of operating without direct human control.

combine
A harvesting machine featuring different attachments, or heads, to harvest different crops.

cover crop
A crop planted on a field between commercial crop seasons, such as in the winter.

economies of scale
The cost savings companies gain by increasing production.

furrow
A groove made in a field into which seed is placed.

genotyping
The process of figuring out a DNA sequence.

geopolitics
The way in which geography, economics, and population distribution affect politics.

Global Positioning System (GPS)
A system that uses the timing of signals from orbiting satellites to determine the precise location of a receiver on Earth.

input
The materials required for a farmer to begin production, including pesticides, fertilizer, seeds, and feed.

irrigation
A system that brings water from one location to an area that has crops.

machine learning
A type of artificial intelligence that enables computers to learn from data without specific programming.

photosynthesis
The chemical process in which plants convert sunlight, water, and carbon dioxide into oxygen and energy in the form of sugar.

spectral imagery
Combining photography with other technologies to gather and analyze data from wavelengths outside the range of human vision.

synthetic
Produced in a lab using chemicals.

volatilize
To cause to evaporate.

yield monitor
An add-on to a harvesting machine that measures and reports yields in real time.

SELECTED BIBLIOGRAPHY

"GMO Basics." *GMO Answers*, 2021, gmoanswers.com. Accessed 21 May 2024.

Isabella, J., and S. Hunt. "A Short History of Aquaculture Innovation." *Hakai Magazine*, 24 Aug. 2020, hakaimagazine.com. Accessed 1 Mar. 2024.

Thomas, Heather Smith. "Ranchers Sing the Praises of Mob-Grazing for Cattle." *Beef Magazine*, 28 Feb. 2012, beefmagazine.com. Accessed 16 Mar. 2024.

FURTHER READINGS

Bray, Richard. *Soil Science for Beginners*. Monkey, 2023.

Hogan, Christa. *Food Science*. Abdo, 2025.

Lim, Angela. *The Crop Encyclopedia*. Abdo, 2025.

ONLINE RESOURCES

To learn more about modern farming, please visit **abdobooklinks.com** or scan this QR code. These links are routinely monitored and updated to provide the most current information available.

MORE INFORMATION

For more information on this subject, contact or visit the following organizations:

NATIONAL FFA ORGANIZATION
6060 FFA Dr.
Indianapolis, IN 46278
ffa.org

FFA is an organization for students who are interested in agriculture and want to learn more about careers as farmers, doctors, scientists, teachers, or business owners. It offers resources, scholarships, and learning opportunities.

SUSTAINABLE AGRICULTURE RESEARCH AND EDUCATION (SARE)
University of Maryland
Symons Hall, Rm. 1296
7998 Regents Dr.
College Park, MD 20742
sare.org

SARE offers regional education and grant opportunities to help farmers learn about and implement sustainable agriculture practices. On its website, SARE also offers a wealth of resources and information on topics related to farming and sustainability.

US DEPARTMENT OF AGRICULTURE (USDA)
1400 Independence Ave. SW
Washington, DC 20250
usda.gov

The USDA provides information on food, commercial and livestock farming, food safety, and natural resources. It also provides support for families living in rural areas and works to end hunger globally.

SOURCE NOTES

CHAPTER 1. A CROP TAKES SHAPE

1. Kris K. Hirst. "Hunter Gatherers: People Who Live on the Land." *ThoughtCo*, 30 Mar. 2020, thoughtco.com. Accessed 3 Feb. 2024.

2. "Norman Ernest Borlaug." *Encyclopedia Britannica*, 2 Feb. 2024, britannica.com. Accessed 3 Feb. 2024.

3. "US Broiler Performance." *National Chicken Council*, 2023, nationalchickencouncil.org. Accessed 15 Aug. 2024.

4. Grace Galler. "Expert Predicts AI Fueled 'Fourth Agricultural Revolution.'" *New Food Magazine*, 9 Jan. 2024, newfoodmagazine.com. Accessed 3 Feb. 2024.

5. "What Are the World's Most Important Staple Foods?" *WorldAtlas*, 2024, worldatlas.com. Accessed 10 Feb. 2024.

6. "Union Farms: How a Leading Pork Producer Achieves Carbon Neutrality in the Name of Sustainability." *GS1*, 2023, gs1us.org. Accessed 4 Feb. 2024.

CHAPTER 2. HYBRID GENETICS AND GMOS

1. "Fast Facts about Agriculture & Food." *American Farm Bureau Federation*, n.d., fb.org. Accessed 22 Mar. 2024.

2. "How Are Corn Hybrids Created?" *YouTube*, 4 Sept. 2015, uploaded by University of Nebraska Lincoln, youtube.com. Accessed 11 Feb. 2024.

3. "Genetically Modified Organisms 101." *GMO Answers*, 2021, gmoanswers.com. Accessed 11 Feb. 2024.

4. "Mary-Dell Chilton History Project Interview, Part I." *Vimeo*, uploaded by GES Center, NC State, 17 Feb. 2016, vimeo.com. Accessed 20 Mar. 2024.

5. Gwendolyn Bogard. "Agrobacterium: Nature's Genetic Engineer, Hidden within Plant Tumors." *Golden Goose Award*, 2023, goldengooseaward.org. Accessed 20 Mar. 2024.

CHAPTER 3. PRECISION AGRICULTURE

1. "Fast Facts about Agriculture & Food." *American Farm Bureau Federation*, n.d., fb.org. Accessed 22 Mar. 2024.

2. Peter Liebhold. "The Crop of the 21st Century." *Smithsonian National Museum of American History*, 16 July 2018, americanhistory.si.edu. Accessed 17 Feb. 2024.

3. "Broadband." *US Department of Agriculture*, n.d., usda.gov. Accessed 14 Mar. 2024.

4. "Irrigation Techniques." *US Geological Survey*, 2 Dec. 2016, water.usgs.gov. Accessed 17 Feb. 2024.

5. "Agricultural Remote Sensing Basics." *North Dakota State University*, n.d., ag.ndsu.edu. Accessed 17 Feb. 2024.

6. Madeleine Baerg. "Real-Time Kinematic Technology Use and Costs." *Grainews*, 19 Mar. 2021, grainews.ca. Accessed 23 Mar. 2024.

CHAPTER 4. MODERN FARM EQUIPMENT

1. "Farming and Farm Income." *US Department of Agriculture Economic Research Service*, 2024, ers.usda.gov. Accessed 18 Feb. 2024.

2. Daniel Munch. "Grain Storage Capacity Can Buffer Impact of Transportation Disruptions." *American Farm Bureau*, 20 Oct. 2023, fb.org. Accessed 14 Mar. 2024.

3. "Autonomous Tractors: Pros and Cons for Farmers in 2023." *AgTecher*, 9 Nov. 2023, agtecher.com. Accessed 18 Feb. 2024.

4. Courtney Perrett. "First Autonomous Tractor Arrives at MU." *University of Missouri*, 5 Sept. 2023, showme.missouri.edu. Accessed 17 Feb. 2024.

5. "Farming and Farm Income."

6. "Drones on the Farm in 2023." *YouTube*, uploaded by Aerial Influence, 20 Dec. 2022, youtube.com. Accessed 17 Feb. 2024.

7. "Drones on the Farm."

8. Bill Knudson. "Results of the Dairy Employment Survey." *Michigan State University*, n.d., canr.msu.edu. Accessed 18 Feb. 2024.

9. "National Agricultural Workers Survey 2019–2020 Selected Statistics." *Farm Worker Justice*, June 2022, farmworkerjustice.org. Accessed 14 Mar. 2024.

10. "How Labor Shortages Are Affecting Agriculture." *Jacksonville Journal-Courier*, 24 Sept. 2023, myjournalcourier.com. Accessed 14 Mar. 2024.

11. "Harvest More Profits." *Produce Grower*, Apr. 2016, producegrower.com. Accessed 18 Feb. 2024.

12. "Strawberry Economics." *Oregon State University Extension*, Oct. 2014, oregonstate.edu. Accessed 18 Feb. 2024.

CHAPTER 5. GROWING AND PROTECTING CROPS

1. Tudi Muyesaier et al. "Agriculture Development, Pesticide Application and Its Impact on the Environment." *International Journal of Environmental Research and Public Health*, vol. 18, no. 3, 27 Jan. 2021, p. 1112, ncbi.nlm.nih.gov. Accessed 4 Mar. 2024.

2. Ned Birkey. "2024 Crop Budgets Are Now Available for Corn and Soybean Budgets." *Farmers Advance*, 16 Nov. 2023, farmersadvance.com. Accessed 14 Mar. 2024.

3. Sharon Raszap Skorbiansky, Andrea Carlson, and Ashley Spalding. "Rising Consumer Demand Reshapes Landscape for US Organic Farmers." *US Department of Agriculture Economic Research Service*, 14 Nov. 2023, ers.usda.gov. Accessed 23 Mar. 2024.

CHAPTER 6. ANIMAL AGRICULTURE

1. John Heggie. "The Future of Livestock Farming." *National Geographic*, 18 Mar. 2019, nationalgeographic.com. Accessed 10 Mar. 2024.

2. Jennifer Ryan. "Getting Ready for Robotic Milking." *Vet Advantage*, Dec. 2020, vet-advantage.com. Accessed 10 Mar. 2024.

3. Samantha Watters. "35-Year Study Shows Trend toward Fewer, Larger Farms." *Maryland Today*, 31 July 2020, today.umd.edu. Accessed 8 Mar. 2024.

4. Watters, "Trend toward Larger Farms."

5. "Who Is the American Farmer?" *USAFacts*, 21 Mar. 2023, usafacts.org. Accessed 8 Mar. 2024.

6. "Cattle/Calf Receipts Make Up Largest Portion of 2022 US Animal/Animal Product Receipts." *US Department of Agriculture Economic Research Service*, n.d., ers.usda.gov. Accessed 9 Mar. 2024.

7. Hannah Ritchie and Max Roser. "Land Use." *Our World in Data*, Sept. 2019, ourworldindata.org. Accessed 8 Mar. 2024.

8. "Fast Facts about Agriculture and Food." *American Farm Bureau Federation*, n.d., fb.org. Accessed 22 Mar. 2024.

9. Heggie, "Livestock Farming."

10. Uduak Thomas. "CRISPRd Pigs: Precision Porcine Gene Editing Combats PRRS Virus Threat." *GenEngNews.com*, 14 Feb. 2024, genengnews.com. Accessed 8 Mar. 2024.

11. "Enteric Fermentation." *Climate and Clean Air Coalition*, n.d., ccacoalition.org. Accessed 16 Mar. 2024.

12. "Bovaer." *DSM-Firmenich*, 2024, dsm.com. Accessed 16 Mar. 2024.

CHAPTER 7. CEA SYSTEMS

1. Liz Kang. "Is the Biggest Greenhouse in the US the Future of Farming?" *CNN*, 6 Oct. 2021, cnn.com Accessed 18 Feb. 2024.

2. Claudia Sisomphou. "The Life of Lettuce." *Sonoma State University*, 25 Sept. 2017, cce.sonoma.edu. Accessed 16 Mar. 2024.

3. Wilfried Aulbur and Giovanni Schelfi. "Can CEA Be a Significant Contributor to Addressing Sustainable Food Production?" *Roland Berger*, 5 June 2023, rolandberger.com. Accessed 28 Feb. 2024.

4. "Vertical Farming: No Longer a Futuristic Concept." *US Department of Agriculture Agricultural Research Service*, 12 July 2023, ars.usda.gov. Accessed 1 Mar. 2024.

5. "Agrivoltaics: Coming Soon to a Farm Near You?" *US Department of Agriculture Climate Hubs*, n.d., climatehubs.usda.gov. Accessed 8 Mar. 2024.

6. Lilah Burke. "Are These Vertical Farm-Grown Luxury Strawberries the Future of Fruit?" *Vegetarian Times*, 19 May 2022, vegetariantimes.com. Accessed 8 Mar. 2024.

7. Aulbur and Schelfi, "Can CEA Be a Significant Contributor?"

8. Emma Bryce. "Are We Ready for Indoor Wheat?" *Anthropocene Magazine*, 31 July 2020, anthropocenemagazine.org. Accessed 16 Mar. 2024.

9. Aulbur and Schelfi, "Can CEA Be a Significant Contributor?"

10. Aulbur and Schelfi, "Can CEA Be a Significant Contributor?"

11. "Tide to Table Profile: Superior Fresh." *National Oceanic and Atmospheric Administration Fisheries*, 25 Sept. 2023, fisheries.noaa.gov. Accessed 1 Mar. 2024.

12. "Revol Greens Further Expands Its New Texas Greenhouse Adding 10 Acres, Increasing Output by 50%." *AgriTechTomorrow*, 17 Nov. 2023, agritechtomorrow.com. Accessed 27 Feb. 2024.

13. Jasmine Lotts. "Texas Welcomes World's Largest Controlled Environment Agriculture Lettuce Facility." *KWTX*, 31 May 2023, kwtx.com. Accessed 27 Feb. 2024.

CHAPTER 8. REGENERATIVE AGRICULTURE

1. "Fast Facts about Agriculture and Food." *American Farm Bureau Federation*, n.d., fb.org. Accessed 22 Mar. 2024.

2. "Conventional Tillage: Moldboard Plow." *North Carolina State Extension*, n.d., soilmanagement.ces.ncsu.edu. Accessed 16 Mar. 2024.

3. Ken Roseboro. "Indiana Farmer Rick Clark." *Green America*, Mar./Apr. 2019, greenamerica.org. Accessed 8 June 2024.

4. "Frequent Questions about US Biogas Projects." *US Environmental Protection Agency*, 2024, epa.gov. Accessed 8 Mar. 2024.

5. "Meet Rick Clark." *Farmer's Footprint*, n.d., farmersfootprint.us. Accessed 8 June 2024.

JILL C. WHEELER

Jill C. Wheeler is a farm kid from Iowa and the author of more than 200 nonfiction titles for young readers. Her interests include behavioral sciences, sustainable agriculture, and any kind of travel. She lives in Minneapolis, Minnesota, with her husband, an overly social dog, and a dangerously affectionate cat.